The Political Romantic

The Political Romantic:
TALES OF A BRONX BOY

BRYAN CORNEL ISA MUHAMMAD FOX

Copyright © 2017 by Bryan Fox

All rights reserved. No part of this publication may be reproduced, distributed, or transmitted in any form or by any means, including photocopying, recording, or other electronic or mechanical methods, without the prior written permission of the publisher, except in the case of brief quotations embodied in critical reviews and certain other noncommercial uses permitted by copyright law. For permission requests, write to the publisher, addressed "Attention: Permissions Coordinator" at the address below.

First Printing, 2017

Paperback ISBN   978-0-9992784-0-6
eBook ISBN   978-0-9992784-1-3

The Hodge Agency
thehodgeagency@gmail.com
www.thehodgeagency.com

Ordering Information:
Quantity sales. Special discounts are available on quantity purchases by corporations, associations, and others. For details, contact the publisher at the address above.

Orders by U.S. trade bookstores and wholesalers. Please contact Big Distribution: Tel: (202) 491-9643; or visit www.thehodgeagency.com.

Printed in the United States of America

Truth

cuts more throats than a politician

Junkie

Give me heaven

Give me life

Give it to me

I want it all

till I can't get anymore

Then I want more

even if you don't get none

none at all

It's all for me

all of it

the demons along with it

I want hell

Give me hell

Give me the pain

I want it

I need it

to fill

this empty

space

That Life: Rain, Sleet, Snow, Sunshine

Winter

snow, coke

blowing, falling, packing

heat, hustlers, skin, women

swimming, singing, swinging

hips, bikini's

summer

Land of the Free

In concrete jungles ghetto choir directors move their hands and make the rebels sing

gunshots ring. Carnegie Hall symphonies

are produced by infamous criminals. High school graduation rates

are at a bare minimum like our current wage. Fearful men display

tough images, survival of the fittest. Crew versus crew marching in cadence

till blood spills, and bodies

outlined in white chalk by the boys in blue. Welcome

to the land

of the free

Projects

Projects

Experiments

Implemented by dead

Presidents, roaches, blow, concrete

Jungles

Mother

Mother

Giver of life

Consumed by self-hatred

Generational dysfunction

Begins

Monsters

Monsters

Lacking love from

Those who were supposed to

Care. Sadness, madness, savage wreaks

Havoc

No Love

I damn near be on death row for that

rose, that

morning dew got her

opening up. I'm trying to be on some'in

soakin' it up. Hands we

throwing them up like

one for this thing called

life

I gots my dark side nigga face it

I'm selfish as fuck I know you hate it. I won't lie

I never learned how to be a man. All I know how

to do is survive, like

one for the rage dem

niggas feelin' like

animals in a cage dem

young bucks wit a twenty two

gage dem

savages wreak

havoc. Haven't you got any fuckin

clue what

What it's like when you gets no

love

Chances of staying alive feelin like

one outta ten, razor blades out the mouth, sharp

tongues makin' monsters outta

men

Fear No One

I wish you'd try and bring me pain. I'm a bona fide psych patient, got no patience. I go

insane

berserk, ballistic, animalistic straight cannibalistic. I'll eat your jugular vein

I be

like Ali

when his back was against the ropes in

Zaire

I fear

no one

Gin Martini

Straight to hell I'll send thee wit a one way ticket
I roll wit badd bitches that's my niggas. They hurt
like this verse, pit bulls in skirts dutch splittin'
take a puff pause for a minute, then look at the
ground, and right back at ya blouw! Charlie's
Angel's hitman
Bet you'd like to hit em'
They look at you like you trippin'
Bipolar shit flippin', crazy sexy and cool chillin' for
a while, then straight flippin'
again, like Beijing's gymnasts, pupils elliptic, ice
Olympic
Ultimate penetration watch these queens conquer
you going feel it
Behold the realist
female assassins on some ill shit

Pussy

Pussy

Tallies made of

Dicks, lick, to reach Mecca

The center of the lollipop

Revered

She Hulk

Gucci

wearing

dudes be

staring

middle fingers up, is how much she be caring

Mike Tyson hits

when she walk through the door

all them dudes hit the floor

James Bond, 007, assassin shit

I love the way she blow the smoke

off the nine

millimeter. You know

when you meet her, fuck with her and she meaner

than juggernaut

and got more brawn than Lance Armstrong

For her cats is no competition.

She got a razor tongue that cut more throats

than a politician

You listen

when she talk

because she on that political statement making

She forever paper chasing

mean

green

money making machine. She the Incredible

She Hulk

Swag so Black

Buy the dutch

Buy the swag

Swag like piff

Swag like diesel

Diesel for me

Diesel for my dawgs

Dawgs for life

Dawgs till the day I die

Die hard

Die happy

Happy times

Happy eyes

Eyes weary

Eyes red

Red zone

Red lights

Lights flashing

Lights out

Out of inhibition

Out to fight

Fight the oppressor

Fight the system

System is flawed

System is broken

Broken promises

Broken laws

Laws in place

Laws perpetuate hate

Hate kills us inside

Hate kills the vibe

Vibe to Bob Marley

Vibe to the rebels

Rebels for cause

Rebels for change

Change in perspective

Change in ways

Ways we live

Ways we think

Think like Malcolm X

Think like a leader

Leader with character

Leader for justice

Justice for the land

Justice for the people

People that are Brown

People that are Black

Black lives

Black bodies

Bodies

Lives

RAGING

Raging

Sticks, stoned, blunts, bone

Bats, knives, take lives, mirror

Lies, die young inside, fly corpses

Empty

Chains

The allure of it all, the cars, the broads walking by

American trucks looking inside heavens doors

What's it all for

You think Satan ain't waitin' on ya ass

But I don't give a fuck, I want what I want and I'm goin' have

None of you mothafuckaz could tell me jack

It pays to be cray. Bring a knife, bring some bats, and a gat cuz we goin' scrap

I'm forever broken nothing could save me. Who you comin' fo? You bout to see what Imma do to you

I'm true to you

cuz what else is there to live for? I'm feeling like there's no hope

I'm jaded and chasin' everythin' outside myself tryin' to fill up somethin' inside me like I'll never be whole

Fear

A white woman

Clenches her husband by his forearm

When a Black male

Wearing a hoodie

Walks by

One Up

If there ain't nothing in it for me then I ain't in it

Whatever you think in your righteous mind that I need to hear, I won't hear it

I rather listen

out for false information and your insecurities to gain ammunition

I came through the gates of hell forgive me in advance for my self-seeking advances I'm afflicted

I carry my past around in smelly garbage bags, shits getting old but my references tell me people ain't shit

So I have a bad tendency to stick to what I know and never let cats get too close

I keep it cool, and remain aloof like

you come one step further and you gettin' the boot

Weapons

Weapons

Use of deadly

Blunt force trauma, razor

Sharp tongues, point blank range, blame, aim, pull

Trigger

Fa da Boom Bap's Sake

You goin know me like the back of your palm
when you feel the fury of the back of my palm.
When I raise this arm
it be in ya best interest to disarm all arms
You don't wanna did no start none
I know cats that won't hesitate to go rati-tat-tat
that's one for the rage. I put pens to a page and
that boom bap
Niggas be like, who dat?, like, you rap? Somethin
fi all dat energy
and all my frenemies
they smile in my face but on Facebook ain't
friends wit me
Have me actin' wild tryin to figa it all out
Obsessions put me in the school of hard knocks
had to learn dem lessons
Yeah I went crazy over many broads

But don't get it twisted, this tongue of mine gifted come before any broad

Cuz to think I'll hurt or do dirt to get back at her and in the end I'll be left mo hurt?

What's worse

Maybe I'm cursed and art is a form of self-expression so I write shit fuck three times between them lines

Bet you luh dis

Take ya jury shoot em in they eyes before they could judge this

Curse

My karma waiting like the curses my ancestors
probably bestowed upon me, Santeria beads
I'm finna get tattoos in all the worst places, and I
stay cuttin' up my arm tryin' to make my soul
bleed just so I can feel anything
Uncle J took his own life like it's in my blood to
wanna see my blood maybe that's why I'm so
numb
on the inside, the hurt can't see it in my eyes, the
ink's my tears, how I face my fears. Bitches be like
damn nigga you could write
and I be like, yeah, you right, bet, you like, like
I'm one of a kind getting' real ree ree off them
trap boom bap beats fi sheezy. I'm outta my mind
Vicious verses grippin' ya soul get ya chin tapped if
you try to take a at jab me, like a rubberband
watch how I snap back it's only a matter of time

before you be feelin' the hate. I came straight through hells gates. Aim fa ya head dot on ya face is how I spell "fuck you." pen straight to the page

Here's Ya Two Cents

A stranger told me

Make lemonade from lemons

I pissed on his face

Comfort Food

"Dyke"

"Freak"

"Creep"

"Yo, you just had sex"

"Why you walk that way"

"Something wrong with your fuckin face"

"Why you talk that way"

It's funny how you become so familiar with hate

like a coward's dick. Young girls overweight

with whom predatory men overstay

they welcome

preying on young girls and saying they here

to help them

They mislead

plant seeds

to grow food

so that poison

becomes their go to

Masks

I couldn't be too sweet, I'd be eaten alive

Thrown to the wolves unhealed wounds turn to

God sized holes

I wore rage like armor in order to survive

Shade blocks light of the spirit, windows to my

soul

Perfectionist

I'm

A caged

Animal

Trapped in my mind

Petrified of my own humanity

Show me Love

I missed the school bus because my mother woke up late. She kicked me in my stomach and slapped me 'cross my face

I fell down to the floor and she kicked me some more. She kept hittin' me

She told me tell them lies so ACS wouldn't find out no one w'd listen to me

She knocked the screws loose can barely keep my head straight. I learned early how ta spread hate through my mouth, like an ak-47 my words spray

God forbid you come incorrect wanna make you shed tears

I'm losing my mind to find my soul and face my fears. I ain't perfect, actin' out hopin' you'll say "I'm thinkin'a u"

If you had my life you'd come out to gate swingin' too

So luh me, don't fuckin judge me. I don't care who you are ain't nobody above me

Poets

Poets

Tormented souls

Hearts bleeding out through pen

Soldiers conquering the uni-

Verses

Give it my All

Through the ink in my pen I bleed pain. I was six when my mother started beating rage into my veins. Don't you dare say my name in vain
Love my weakness I ain't get enough, all I know is hate
So on some Jake LaMotta shit
I be swingin', I be swingin' like I on't deserve ta lih
It's the mentality of this modern day Bronx bull
My head got knocked round and I got lots of loose screws. If I were you
I'd put an end to that shit you pull. I'm on my Biggie shit if ya ain't know now ya know
to the fullest I'm reppin E. Gun Hill Road
Mothers crying when they children slain
Policies of dead presidents, put holes in our souls, so we started puttin' holes in each other's membranes
Politicians never gave a fuck, fucked us over n' out

This the shit white folk will never know bout.
Untamed youth speak with hand gestures
imitations of guns bussin' back, how we honor our
founding fathers and dead presidents. Lyndon B Johnson
turned Black folk to projects making monsters outta men
We don't have much but a madd verse bro
Life some badd words shits a curse yo. From 174th
to Yankee Stadium and 161st so
better get your game right. When the Yanks ain't
playing it's game night. Tonight for my peeps
shrimp linguini pasta
My dawgs happy, take a toke, blow the smoke,
hittin' blunts like they Rasta. I keeps my circle
tight n you's an imposter
You tryin' stop me, bih please, don't even bother
I'm wit my peeps havin' fun. Nonstop all night to
till we see the sun

I'm a compassionate soul, in dem hataz eyes I see my son
that's one
for the BX where youngin's be slingin' guns
I need you to throw yo hands up
like you surrenderin' to me and my wrath I reign
on this mic, terror. Young pharaoh
I'm special ed epic top of my class makin' no errors
Behold a new me I've been resurrected
my style eclectic. To whom is you steppin, best gets to steppin. Hit em' in they ear with that hook, a loopin' left n left'em
Over you there ain't a day in my life I'll be stressin'. Take a look inside
the life of this Reagan grandchild, hear our cries, no more profiting off of our demise

A Tribute to Those Lost in a New York Minute

Part I

New York night lights fast pace, increased heart rate and heart ache

The night life, the dark side, it's the internal fight to stay alive

The city that never sleeps

the silenced that won't dare to speak

up. The unjust.

Your mind, need to unwind, the grind, got no time to waste, no mistakes, hop on that train, try to stay sane

No slowing. Keep it goin' off to no where real early

Youth coming up real early, grandparents in they thirties, needle looking really dirty

Even though you try to stay clean, HIV, you can't even see

how time fly before you could ask yourself why, or who, when, where, how. You barely experiencing the now

A Tribute to Those Lost in a New York Minute

Part II

New York City skyline, supported by high rises, high crime continues to prevail with the onset of tough times

Gotta move at God's speed to eat, even on a don't walk sign, got no time to waste

A young mother's section eight apartment's at stake

She sells her body and her soul for the cash she make

Everyday it's a constant battle for her to mask the shame

No matter how much her curves swerve up in the lime light

and she work upside down on that pole so her daughter could shine bright

brighter than the dim project night lights, self-hatred inside her. Blush, make-up, and eye liner, got her sniffing white lines to get higher

than the Manhattan skyscrapers to reach the heavens above

Through her encounters with men she wondering if she'll ever meet her true love

A Tribute to Those Lost in a New York Minute

Part III

I'm The Bronx warrior, so I wear the stories of the New Yorker's

on my shirt, New York City's number one reporter

At night rats clickety clack clack, scratching up the insides of project walls

During the day rats cut back on taxes towards school funds down in city hall

New York

is the place where people know very well not to listen to slick politicians

in this world of fly girls and cut throat competition

among the Wall Street brokers

This the reason why the poor get broker

Major class division from the two-bedroom splitting houses in Huguenot

Staten Island, to the projects in Stapleton. Money maker men selling rock

The suburban like white picket fence homogeny in Queens,

to the white lines splitting, measuring quarter keys

in the Queensbridge projects, noxema

In these grimy streets of New York, you won't find anything cleaner

From the Brownstones in Park Slope Brooklyn to the projects in Brownsville Crooklyn

the claim cultural center of diversity seems to be an absurdity. You know why there ain't any doormen past 103rd street no maids, expensive cars, or Whole Foods markets, only the University

buying up Harlem's apartments without any consideration

There's no negotiations for gentrification just kick them to the curb

They'll learn how to earn a decent living, resorting to violence to overcome oppressed silence

in The Bronx where crime rate is at its highest. Summer time, open fire hydrants

is where we throw our X's up, welcome

to my hard knock city the place where the Timberland boot gritty

thugs, with manes in braids call all the shots

Kings of these urban jungles, animals caged, in abandoned buildings and vacated lots

These are the people that the Ronald Reagan's, Trump's, and Bush administrations

forgot

Poison

Poison

Worlds most hated

Dare to be my true self

Taint Colonial concepts with

Blackness

Conditions

Love

I was

Told is not

Conditional

But all that changed when I changed my gender

How the Suit's Stitched

I can't live my life to

suit you

So instead I get Italian suits

custom made and measured

to suit me

Road to Recovery

I

Try to

Reach the sky

With my feet still

planted on the ground. It's so hard to learn

Quickie

Coffee with my sugar, seven in the morn, flowers mourn
I'm familiar with that rose when it's weeping
Sleepy tongues unite, mouths open wide, party up in here, the funk
Serve me some'in sunny side up
then flip it again
Got me yoking, tie loosened, let's lose control and go in on that snooze button, ooze button, rosebuds succulent
Legs scrambled, must read that AA preamble
I promise we'll finish just ten more minutes.
Nonstop moving to the rhythm
and the rhyme
I could barely get to work on time

Pie

I

love

Americano baby

that three

point one four

apple truffles and

vanilla ice cream

She got

the power

weeping

flower

on my mind

and my tongue

action

This is class

crass

fractions

a piece

at a time

till she reach

satisfaction

My Favorite Vice

Your bittersweetness, strawberries and

vinaigrette scents between legs

like dots between letters, sealed with your

tongue, that this mail man been delivered

straight to

your liver

Slivers, quicker, slicker, quivers, heavy, hitter

I'm a dope fiend in between bed sheets, wet like

flipper

Michael Phelps, Olympic swimmer

Your ballet dance on my diving board, got my

body sprung off this headboard. You like that

monkey on this addicts back, the way you

squeeze me

tease me

Best believe me

when I say

don't you ever

leave me

Hypnotic

Her eyes

are hypnotic

one glance

and I lose

my mind

She a Loui Vuitton bitch with the matching

shoes, a true

fucking New Yorker, and

I'm just a lost cause along for the ride, following

the curves of her eye lashes moving upward and

to the side like

the j line

swerving

d.w.i.'s

At this point of intoxication, back

there's no turning

This train is barreling and I can't stop pushing

this thing

forward

I'm lost

in the bliss

I'm lost

Her eyes

are so

hypnotic

Manual

She said "I love the way you move it

like it's one with you"

I said I'm a natural at driving stick

Mind Fuck

You can't see it

but it's there

You can feel it

soul deep

when I speak

to you

My words make Freudian slips

tapping into places

you never imagined

Fatal Attraction

I like how you're so

submissive like that sweet

surrender a king pin yields when it's game

over, like that time you got

got and loved every

moment of it, like the time we

smashed in a South Bronx

alley, like that time we

hit the Major Deegan Bridge and went over

the edge

The Morning After

I

Really

Love the way

You throw your hands

Up in the air and say His name in vain

Love Addiction

She stuck with me spinning round and round on this Ferris wheel. Love is my Achilles heel
I felt like I never got enough, seemed like every flower I'd find I crush. Self-fulfilling prophecy
I became the monster my mother told me I was destined to be
said I was too ugly and no one'd ever wanna touch me
To break this cycle I tried so hard
Felt like Sasquatch, Bowser, or King Kong
like ya Seen me on the top floor with some white women, and they some fine women, eyes like Sierra Leone's diamonds
The haterz couldn't stand it tried to be on some biggie shit "who shot ya"
But love the bombs and bullets couldn't stop me from having you in the grip of my palm like "who gotcha"

Beauty just leave my side, before I decide to never let you go for eternity like the length of this instrumental

Do yourself a favor while I have the mercy to let you go with all my might, runaway before I change my mind, and spare your mental

well-being from my massive insecurities manifested in the form of possessiveness, you're my dopamine

This what lack of love will do to you, and with or without you feel like there's no hope for me

Mary Jane

I'm done with the booze and hard drugs, but she still get the best of me
She home to the lost causes, blowing in the wind like tobacco from split Phillies
I'm done with lusting, but when she roll the blunt with her tongue I luh them wet willies
No sex with me, I just want her to lay next to me
Get in bed with me. You just got here and now you finna leave
I never knew how much my best friend could be my worst enemy

BPD (borderline personality disorder)

My mood slide, up and down like the moons tides. On the pendulum of my emotions

I'm left hook swinging like jazz eighth notes roller coasting

No straights I detour, life on a seesaw

I'm merry-go-round turning like a stripper's curves swerving

I'm a tornado, direction hard to pin it, coin flipping hit or miss it

like these veins to numb these pains. Attention seeking, screaming

at the top of my lungs with a razor in my hand, blade to my wrist

hoping that this scratch will take care of the itch. Wild manic and dramatic like the titanic. Unfortunately for some these actions lead to a very tragic

aftermath. Shit sound like the Oscars except this ain't no acting class. All of the sudden

someone push that one button, rage turn into a bloodbath. Shit got me feeling like why the fuck God made me

this way, trapped in my mind's a prison and I can't escape feelin' crazy

Although you can't hear me, I'm yelling on the inside

Depression sets in gotta drag ass through the day just to get by

I'll cut you to say I love you and when you leave, I'll say fuck you

I'm torn between past and future and don't know the now. Intimate relationships, I don't know the how

to get shit through to you

Even when I'm conniving and deceitful I'm true to you

Love Will Kill You

in the ring

So when you feelin' her, act like it ain't nothing

As soon as you get real they always go running

Ya best bet is to let EA sports come out the mouth

because it's all in the game keep frontin'

Keep yo chest out, keep cool, keep struttin'

What they hate they love and to want who don't want us is human nature

I tried to keep my guard up but I couldn't take her

She touch me it's a rap jack. How many times I fell for that I can't even remember

Before you know it my heart stuck in a blender

And just like that she gone way past November

So I keep my reach long range, and keep her arms at bay

Like don't hug me baby, wanna make you love me baby, I wish I could make these feelings go away

Before I could even look, I'll fall in love with her

that one left hook that got me down for the count

and I'll never recover

Passing Storm

Could see her body silhouette in clouds that's wispy
I put the booze down only to find a different kind of whisky
In my ear she softly whispering
All over my neck she kissing me
Ernesto Quinonez bodega dreams
I wonder if she could feel this roll of quarters, bodega feign like
hit me off with two loosies and a dutch, bed sheets clutched
Method Man sugar walls coming down baby you been touched
Checked the clouds through dense fog I know I can feel that summer rain
That light mist that comes with a little bit of pain
This Jones in my bones to jump your bones you can feel it in your veins

And just like that you were gone, a passing storm

It's so real, so ill how I swore you were in my arms

SOUL CRY

Soul cry

Body wilting

Yellow tulips wither

Without light, dull eyes, someone, please

Love me

Like Mother like Son

"You don't wanna be with me, then I wanna die f'real"
My mother's ex told her "go head, kill yourself, kill your kids it ain't goin' to change how you feel"
It's funny how I ended up followin' in her footsteps. She always told me to go back to my room when all I ever wanted to do was connect
I went back in my mind where everything was so great, while she ate ice cubes, took a few puffs of her cig, and looked away
I planned my escape and ran, far far far away to a place where I couldn't feel the pain. No more rain
It was picture perfect weather never land
Ice cubes in a bong, bloodshot red eyes staring back at me in the mirror, years later look at where I stand

I put away the dank, now I'm using human beings to rage and clinging to you hoping that I can feel safe

Romantic obsession got me going insane compromising my self-respect. I be wondering what the fuck it'll take

How many "I don't give a fucks?" could set this fucker straight for the love of fuckin' God motha fuckin' fucks sake. How many heart breaks

How can I put love out there in the world if I don't know how to go within

I just pick up this pen and bleed out all this hurt in a verse hoping one day I'll fall in love with myself again

Fathers

Fathers

Kings led astray

By worldly distractions

Fail to provide for their loved ones

Missing

Human Dildo

I'm feeling worthless, as if

that Facebook relationship status is equivalent to

what is known as the elite upper echelon, and

single or quote on quote just friends is

peasantry level. I'm not in the

game. I'm sitting on the

sidelines because I'm second rate, straight

entry level

I'm not

it, like I'm not

getting it, like "yo

my dude

you wasn't

getting it

last night"

Here's to the Broken

I draw x's over my ex's pics, cig to the sky blowing o's like
the holes in my soul. I know how to put on a show, but my smile is a little outta place
I took after my mother lookin' for love in the wrong place
Imma lost cause back in high school after I finished my class work used to roam dem halls
Now I'm twenty eight, tattoos fi every heart break, rip my flesh open to ease the pain, in this world still tryin find my way
Fa all the bonds I broke my karma waitin' for me it's time to pay
up. But till that day I be throwin' my hands way up, doin my thing across the stage, across the page. I'm hoping to get my cake up that's one for the rage
and one fa the cage

my beautiful dark mind where all the negativity is engraved

I don't know what I'm worth. I wonder sometimes why God put me on this earth

The answer lies right before my eyes, feel my pain when I bleed ink I give you my word

Deja Vu

I'm the devils tongue searing through south Bronx

windows back in the seventies, barren wastelands

The crack era, cuts in funding for education

at the hands of Reagan, 88' man, devastation

My verses reign terror like baby face killers

dumpin' clips

on loose lips, sinking ships, torrential downpours.

Hurricane tidal waves, gats wave, when it rains it

pours

This that flow that bring cats to they knees

like pipes do to a crack feign. Gats scream, the

smash team

spray like open fire hydrants at night

patron n' bar fights throwing all that water in ya

face. Spit fire like

it's the seventies all over again. Pretend you

control the rage, decades of pain like

modern day slaves, Black lives displaced,

politicians raid our land for the betterment of they

own kind call it the Bronx Expressway

Look a nigga in the eye, get caught out there, with

the cross Bronx Expressway straight to ya face like

niggas ain't the Yanks. Out here there ain't no

time to play games. Welfare lines, teenage

mother's a disgrace

to the Latino machismo mentality, and all that

virgin Mary shit

Obey the Father, keep a closed mouth, keep

closed lips

priests and preachers preachin' closed mouths

don't get fed. Ladies

obey the father. Young boys lustin' over broad

hips, it would be an honor

if I can hit that, like, if I can hit it, women

becoming punching bags for young men of color,

using hyper-masculinity as armor

misguided and they insecurities run

riot like the desks and chairs thrown out the

windows of schools. Gang turf n' crooks without

borders, whatchu thought a teacher ever going to

have any order

This is our world we livin', zero fuckin' fucks given,

if the system is rigged, politicians go fishing

for more young Black lives to fulfil their status

quo, tokens just to gain more votes and

We left hung out to dry on some modern day

lynchin'

Focus

Limp loosies used to have me tight like, I tried lightin' em' up but I froze
When a little Debbie walked by, I stood tall shorty right up under my nose
I tossed the shit so I can say hello
tryina come across wild mellow, but bitches think Pakistan is in the hizzouse, be like nah I'm just wild yellow
Nigga light-skinned always play the field. I wanna score these numbaz but my game on half-time tryna smash time like
how I used to put away Rum 150 back in the day
I gave her the nod
and she looked away, then looked back, gave me screw-face. Say
Ms. Gin Martini is a gritty broad

Come to thinkin' I need to start thinkin' broad, cuz my peeps gotta eat time to get dumb smart, crazy tactful the way I pursue the arts
Niggaz can't get enough of these lines, you'd think my verses dope, give feigns hope, when I pour out my heart. Team rrrahh! Right? Like
Moofasa, who gotcha? X marks the mothafuckin' spot son
and all dem other letters that I put together to make a magnificent show
To all my people you my poppauncbros, till the day it's time for me to go

Dopeless Hopefiend

Helpless

Hopeless

Drugless

Dopeless

I was a helpless hopeless dopefiend

Now I'm a drugless dopeless hopefiend

Serenity

Hell

Mind, state

Raving, raging, burning

Inside, dark, light, fight

Drinking, swinging, sinking

Surrender, change

Heaven

Joy

makes me feel so light,

through the dark and lonely nights

I'll keep up the fight.

Until I Find Her

I'm searching

across the seven seas

of broken hearts

The Prowl

Severe clear blue skies...

A woman's dress blew up, while

walking down the street.

May Lady

You like severe clear skies some'in like seventy five degrees
Imma be sincere dear all I can think bout is the birds and the bees
You charismatic, the world's most perfect imperfect flower giving much love when you open up
The so called hardest cats crack a smile when you show up
Niggas take long walks round the park they always wanna go with you
like nature wanna grow with you
If you were to ever leave fa good niggaz lose they mind like it's mayday mayhem
Ya warm touch too much the rest of them chicks you slay dem

Rembasquiapicasso how you turn a dark mind like mine into a sunny sky, got the rain petrified of ya

You as close to God as it gets salute to ones that'll die fi ya

Malcolm in the Middle

I'm in the mood. You got me wantin' ta spit a

word or two. I wanna hear somethin' like

she say she'll be my

Ms. May, sweet like Sunday, sun rays, like she say

she'll be mine

Sugar honey sweet cakes

I'll be your chunky monkey beef cake, like

I like my Debbie little, tropical skittles

How this dentist accidentally work his way way up

inside your pelvic cavity

I guess I'm Malcolm in the

middle

Caribbean Thing

Your oxtails in full

swing, it's that

thing that makes me

tick.

You a super

fly

I wonder what's underneath that

sundress. Yeah I'm fresh, fresher than the

ocean breeze Caribbean thing

You my

key lime pie. I love it when you

come in storming, my hurricane, category five

chick

Bonnie and Clyde, be right by my side, till the day I die. It's a Caribbean thing

when you wear

nothing

but the summer rain, when you wear

absolutely

nothing

Tits in the air, one minute I stare, the next

rude boy got you tore up

straight ripping shit

from the floor

up. I lift you up and stick you up like a Caribbean store and

when it rains

it pours, but you my

brown skin, mixed with cinnamon, on which sun be glistening, when you walk by sons be whispering like

that's that Caribbean thing

Sunshine

you mine

You my light, legs crossed, head back, one hell of a sight and

we fight, but

we tight in the midst of

weathering these storms, I look into your eyes, and I know

that everything will be alright

www.ingramcontent.com/pod-product-compliance
Lightning Source LLC
Chambersburg PA
CBHW070544300426
44113CB00011B/1787